THE BEST REVENGE

How to Overcome
Betrayal, Adversity and Abuse

TAWANNA JACKSON-ADAMS

DALLAS, TEXAS

All rights reserved. No part of this book may be reproduced or transmitted in any form or by any means, electronic or mechanical, including photocopying, recording, or by any information storage and retrieval system, without permission in writing from the copyright owner. The views expressed in this work are solely those of the author and do not necessarily reflect the views of the publisher, and the publisher hereby disclaims any responsibility for them.

Copyright © 2021 * Higgins Publishing. All rights reserved.
Tawanna Jackson-Adams * The Best Revenge:
How to Overcome Betrayal, Adversity and Abuse

Scripture taken from the New King James Version®. Copyright © 1982 by Thomas Nelson, Inc. Used by permission. All rights reserved.

THE HOLY BIBLE, NEW INTERNATIONAL VERSION®, NIV® Copyright © 1973, 1978, 1984, 2011 by Biblica, Inc.™ Used by permission. All rights reserved worldwide.

Higgins Publishing supports the rights to free expression and the value of copyright. The purpose of copyright is to encourage writers and artists to produce creative works that enrich our values. The scanning, uploading, and distribution of this book without the express permission of the publisher is a theft of intellectual property. If you would like permission to use material from this book (other than for review purposes), please contact permissions@higginspublishing.com. Thank you for your support of copyright law.

Higgins Publishing | www.higginspublishing.com - The publisher is not responsible for websites (or their content) that are not owned by the publisher. Higgins Publishing is committed to excellence in the publishing industry. The company reflects the philosophy established by the founder, based on Psalm 68:11, 'The Lord gave the word, and great was the company of those who published it.'

Library of Congress Control Number 2021923929 * July 2022

Jackson-Adams Tawanna – The Best Revenge:
How to Overcome Betrayal, Adversity and Abuse

Higgins Publishing – 1st Edition * pcm 80 (PB)

English: 978-1-941580-33-2 (PB) * 978-1-941580-42-2 (E-Book)

(SEL016000) Self-Help: Personal Growth & Happiness
(SEL021000) Self-Help: Motivational & Inspirational
(SOC060000) Social Science: Sexual Abuse & Harassment

For information about special discounts for bulk purchases, subsidiary, foreign, and translations rights, contact Higgins Publishing at sales@higginspublishing.com.

Thank You For Your Purchase. Please Scan the QR Code to post a review at Amazon.

Sign up for Tawanna's newsletter for giveaways, encouragement and free content at TawannaJAdams.com.

~~~

Schedule Tawanna for speaking engagements and virtual tours at TawannaJAdams.com.

Thank you!

Dedication

This book is dedicated to all the children and young adults who are quietly struggling with poverty, neglect, abuse, and chaos in their lives. You, who society has failed by being overlooked, undervalued, and simply ignored! You who have never been asked about your ideas, plans, goals, or dreams. You were told that you would never amount to anything, never do anything or go anywhere. I want to speak to you…yes, you!

Through my life, I want to speak into your life and let you know that you are extremely valuable. My prayer is that *this little girl's* story will encourage you that you, too, can make it! Trials, disappointments, and every other thing that life can throw at you will come, but so will healing, love, and peace when you seek it. God has a purpose for your life…you're not an accident or mistake but made in God's expressed image. My peace, love, and healing all came to me when I embraced God's perfect love for me, knowing that He accepted me, understood me, and had a better plan for me. I also realized that I had to take some responsibility for my life and take control of my emotions, which caused me to make bad decisions based on anger and fear from my past. I had to begin looking outside my current situation and start dreaming again that anything – absolutely anything – was possible for me. Anything is possible for you, too, so begin dreaming again!

I want to encourage you to give yourself permission to enjoy your life. Work on being confident (not arrogant); take your dreams/ideas and get information. Do research, get a mentor, and get empowered! *This little girl* had to get her joy, peace, love, and life back. She did it one step at a time and so can you.

This story is about me, a little girl who, in the beginning, had so much to look forward to, so much time, so many ideas and energy like any other child. Then life came to visit this *girl* and everything changed! This is a recount of events in my life that speak of trials, disappointments, failures, and depression but also of healing, victory, and empowerment. This is not just any story but a testimony! So many of us share similar experiences and don't realize it.

And so, read this book with an open mind. Take some notes along the way and watch God take you from where you are to where He wants you to be!

I dedicate this book to all of you because, like me, you are worth every word. Be encouraged!

TABLE OF CONTENTS

DEDICATION	IV
TABLE OF CONTENTS	VIII
INTRODUCTION	IXX
Chapter One: In The Beginning	1
Chapter Two: Not Me!	5
Chapter Three: Bright Ideas	7
Chapter Four: Living Under Murder Row	11
Chapter Five: Does Crime Ever Pay?	17
Chapter Six: New Jersey, Here We Come Again!	23
Chapter seven: You Might As Well Kill Me!	27
Chapter eight: The Day I Left!	33
Chapter nine: "His Little Girl"	37

TABLE OF CONTENTS

Chapter ten: Life Is Still Worth Living 41

Chapter eleven: This Is Not The Conclusion 45

Chapter twelve: I'm Getting My Voice Back 49

Chapter thirteen: Don't Just Settle 53

Chapter fourteen: My Favorite Bible Story 57

Chapter fifteen: Your Best Revenge! 61

Acknowledgements 65

About the Author 69

INTRODUCTION

The Best Revenge is a book about my struggles growing up, for the most part, without my parents' guidance and support. My brother and I spent many days without food, clean clothes, and the comfort of feeling safe. The book talks about the abuse that I endured for several years from a family member, all while some of my relatives knew and did absolutely nothing to help me. It discusses how the very people who professed to love me turned a blind eye to what was happening, in order to shield the adults who neglected and abused us.

For years, I hated many of them. I couldn't wait to get old enough to say what I really thought of them, and I tried to prove them wrong every chance I got! At times, I wasted my own time, trying to prove something to people who weren't worth the energy. Because of my feelings of hate, disappointment, frustration, humiliation, and depression, I made many bad choices, letting those feelings get in the way of progress! I had to realize that my best revenge wouldn't be achieved through bad behavior and attitude. Rather, it would be achieved by my success!

I had to decide that I was better than what I had been given and that family is defined not solely by blood but also by love. So, I became determined to create a better future for myself by educating myself through school. I deepened my relationship with God through prayer and studying the bible, not just going to church, and I built relationships with others older and wiser than me. This helped me find my way to forgiveness. All of these actions are equally important because each of them made me look at myself and take the focus off everyone else. I stopped blaming!

Finally, I wrote this book while keeping in mind every child and the adult they will become. I don't have all the answers but I do have a few nuggets to help you along your journey. For any adult who, through my testimony, finds their way to forgiving themselves for wasting time and forgiving those who hurt you...you're worth more than the mistakes of others! Find peace, joy, and love. It's here waiting for you, too!

CHAPTER ONE

IN THE BEGINNING

I was born in Dorchester, Massachusetts in 1971, in a neighborhood that was new to my mother because she had just moved there from Newark, New Jersey, where she was born and briefly lived with her biological mother. My mother came to Boston to join Grandma Clark, the person who raised her for most of her childhood. Grandma Clark took my mother in when her mother – my grandmother – contemplated giving her up for adoption because she couldn't afford to take care of her. My mother was always running away from what she thought were her biggest issues there: her mother, my dad, and judgment from family members. Grandma Clark told me that my mother was a beautiful young black woman. Her skin was clear, she had a small frame, and she was so smart and could do anything she set her mind to, including attending Essex Community College. Grandma Clark adored her little piece of "dark chocolate," as she would say. Little did Grandma know that my mom hated that saying and that it would leave her with self-hatred of her skin color throughout her life.

My father was young. During my mother's pregnancy, he was sent to live in Alaska, of all places, with a family member because he was in and out of trouble; at least, that is how his father felt. This was supposed to straighten out his life, to give him a fresh start and, hopefully, a second chance. Well, it did. He met and married his wife and had three children. Unfortunately, I didn't get a chance to enjoy that part of his life because, when I was a child, my mother told me that he was dead. Yup! We'll talk about that later.

My family told me stories about how much my mother loved me, how she would hold me, and how she would talk only to me for hours at a time. I can only imagine how close we were, how I held on to her every word, looking for her all the time. She loved bananas in any form, and so do I!

Life was good even though we didn't have a lot. We lived in a poor part of Dorchester, but it didn't matter then because everyone helped each other. Old ladies would always make themselves available for advice and give cute things to my mom for me. That help came easy for my mom because she was a young mother who had a new baby, and I was the only baby in my family at that time. Then, two years later, my brother came along and the three of us were even closer. We had nicknames, played board games, ran around in the park, and had cookouts – so many fun times together! Life couldn't get much better than that for us. Being surrounded by family was awesome, too! We had family dinners at Grandma Clark's house. She could cook anything and make it taste good. She would store canned food everywhere: closets, cabinets, anywhere she could find a place to put it. We laughed at her but soon her house became a grocery store to us. The lessons she taught my brother and I about sticking together like glue remain with us to this day. Grandma Clark never stopped talking about saving money, managing relationships, getting an education; you name it, she talked about it! The thing is…she wasn't my grandmother by blood but you couldn't tell. She raised my mother from birth, so we all had a special bond.

On the other hand, Grandma Gaston (my biological grandmother), was a woman of few words but her life would speak volumes. That grandma made sure we had fun with her pallets (a stack of blankets and pillows) on the floor. She would tell jokes to make us laugh and cook big meals when she knew we were coming to visit. Grandma Gaston worked very hard to make up for not raising my mother herself by financially supporting my mother. She was as much my friend as she was my grandmother because I could tell her anything and everything! Grandma Gaston shared so much with me as we both got older; some of my best memories are of her. That time with her was amazing! Speaking of her puts a smile on my face and brings tears to my eyes because I miss her the most…my cheerleader! She always told us what she thought was best and she was honest with how she felt about issues and what she called being a realist, which really meant she didn't have very high expectations of anything not to be disappointed. Sometimes, I feel the same way.

The beginning was good, the beginning was loving, the beginning was…just the beginning!

I learned to not be discouraged by how you begin. It's how well you finish!

Job 8:7 "Though your beginning was small, yet your latter end would increase abundantly." (NKJV).

CHAPTER TWO

Not Me!

When I was a young girl, being told all the time that I was going to be just like my mother started as a compliment because I loved my mom so much, she could do no wrong. I believed every word she said and every promise she made. No one could say a bad word about her. However, over time, that statement became an insult to me when I began seeing just what my life would be like living with her! Don't get me wrong; before my mom passed away, to me she was still sixty-four years young, with beautiful black skin and wavy black hair. She was so smart...I wish she knew exactly how my brother and I felt about her, how much she was loved by us. Unfortunately, not dealing with her own issues, she allowed life to beat up on her. She refused to allow pictures to be taken of her ever! She hated the skin she was in. I can only imagine how she felt growing up separated from her birth mother, never knowing who her father was, and not having a good sense of family. I later learned that her drug use was due in part to many unresolved childhood issues. She had her secrets and they left her scarred. Her body told part of the story; you could tell because, at sixty-four, she walked with a walker due to a bad back. She had a list of illnesses that required medications, track marks that covered her body, and a very negative attitude toward everything. She was full of regret. My brother and I had grown to fully forgive her, but she didn't believe it. My mother didn't understand that forgiveness doesn't mean the past will disappear, that suddenly you can re-write history; it means that we can move beyond it. She died alone and that breaks my heart because it didn't have to be like that. We could have moved on if only she had left the past behind. I could not be her; don't let it be you! My advice is to have a healthy sense of regret that will motivate you to change. I have also learned to not become stuck! To not give up! I keep it moving! Philippians 3:13-14 says, "Brothers and sisters, I do not consider myself yet to have taken hold of it. But one thing I do: Forgetting what is behind and straining toward what is ahead, I press toward the goal to win the prize for which God has called me heavenward in Christ Jesus." (NIV).

CHAPTER THREE
BRIGHT IDEAS

My mother, with her bright ideas, wanting to make extra money, was introduced to some of the biggest drug dealers in our neighborhood by none other than a close father-like family friend. It was supposed to be *temporary*, I was told…you know, to buy extra things for us. Back then, when you were on welfare (public assistance), you didn't have anything, and the government intended to keep it that way. So, this was a way to work around the system. Little did my mother know that this idea would be the beginning of a life filled with addiction, crime, and death!

As smart as my mother was, she was also gullible, curious, and greedy. She started selling drugs for these people (a family) and the more she made, the more she wanted to make. These people had leather coats, furs, designer clothes, fancy cars – you name it and she wanted it! Now she already smoked marijuana and drank Nyquil as a teenager. I know this from Grandma Clark's stories. I think that was the easiest way to get high then and probably cheap too! So, the avenue for addiction was present even then. My mom's siblings were already struggling with addiction as well, but she didn't see that because, of course, she was too smart for that! "That will never happen to me." They all thought that way! Then someone came up with the bright idea of using me as one of the kids who would transport drugs and money between locations. No police then even suspected children, so that went on for a few years. It almost seemed normal because it happened so often. They would pack the money around our waists and in our underpants, then tape it so no one would see it. We would then be sent in a cab and, on arrival, knock on the person's door, say the "word" given to us, and be let in – all to have the money removed and the drugs put in their place, then be sent back. You'd think they would feel guilty for using us that way but if they were, they didn't show it. I remember those days like they were yesterday. I was so scared but there was no time for that because we had to be on the lookout.

I don't really know when my mom's bright idea turned into her using drugs, but I remember realizing something was wrong when I was around eight or nine years old. It started with her disappearing all day, then overnight and, afterward, for days on end. We would be so scared, thinking about where she was or if she had overdosed and died. We were always thinking the worst. Then she would come home and make up some fancy story to put our minds at ease. As we got older, sometimes that fear turned into anger. We would complain and talk to each other about what was happening to us and her. She started selling her food stamps, which left us with nothing to eat. Too many times we had no food. Sometimes, I would feel sick and weak from hunger. My brother would keep asking me for food until I would ask a neighbor for something for him to eat, but how many times can you ask? They were on welfare too. So, I started babysitting for my mother's friends and cleaning their apartments so that we could buy food. There were times when these same friends would send me to the store with twenty dollars to get milk, bread, or whatever and let me keep the change to ensure I had money for something to eat. That didn't last long because when my mother got wind of how much her friends were giving me, she would ask to borrow it and always promise to pay it back. I learned very early that "payback" would never happen, but I couldn't say anything to my mother even though I wanted to. You didn't confront this lady and be left intact! Resentment started early for me and lasted way too long.

CHAPTER FOUR

LIVING UNDER MURDER ROW

Murder Row (Sonoma Street) is what most people called the street I grew up on. I'm sure you can imagine what living on a street called Murder Row would be like for a kid. It was sometimes scary because we could peep out the window on any given day and see police paddy wagons lined up along the street and a line of people climbing in. Some nights we could look out and see drug dealers standing on the roofs of the building, watching out for police and rival drug dealers. My brother and I were always told to stay out of the windows, but we were too nosey for that. We looked anyway! But in spite of that we could play outside, skating up and down the street like crazy. As kids, we just ignored our environment for the most part to still have fun.

I remember one summer having a cast on my leg. I had fallen down some stairs while wearing those famous clogs with no rubber on the bottom. What a hot, itchy summer that would be! Oh, but I made the best of it by using one leg to do almost everything that I would usually do with two. After a few weeks, you could find me slipping my cast halfway into a roller skate and skating down the street or racing the other kids down the hill. I wore out the bottom of that cast! Nothing was really left of it except for what managed to survive the tomboy in me. There was no going back to the hospital to have it checked or removed, so I soaked it in the bathtub, took a knife, and sawed it off. What a relief! I could play freely again. For us, there were no regular doctor's appointments - just emergency room visits and being self-sufficient.

There was a wonderful old woman who went to church every Sunday and would call out from her apartment steps: "Who wants to go to church with me"? I would muster up enough courage to start going with her. I didn't really know her, and I would never really know her well, but going to church with her would prove to be a safe place for me. At church, you could sing and dance but, most importantly, eat dinner when service was over. Getting a hot meal was my priority but not my brother's. He would opt to stay outside and play. He would also be hungry those nights, but he should have come to church with me. Going to church with my neighbor was also my first religious encounter. All the prayers, choirs singing, and people jumping up and down looking so happy…I wanted that! Only thing is, I would see folks falling on the floor and others covering them with white sheets and that scared me. I thought they were dead! I would later learn that this was their expression of just how awesome God was in their lives. What could make someone feel full of joy like that? Later in life, I would have my own personal experience with God – one that would fill me with similar joy.

Murder Row was filled with craziness and fun, all of which would become normal to us after a while.

In those days, my brother and I would roller skate or walk from Sonoma Street to East Newton Street, which was about two and a half miles one way, to grocery shop at Grandma Clark's apartment. She would then send us back in a cab, sometimes paying with rolled-up pennies because that was all she had at the time. While we waited for her to pack bags of food for us to take home, she might have us change into oversized t-shirts and shorts so that she could wash our clothes. We would each eat a big hunk of her sweet bread and drink a glass of Kool-Aid. She might have a pot of something good cooking on the stove and we could eat before we went back home. My brother would try to eat as much as he could because he thought that if he ate a lot, it would last longer and keep him from getting hungry too fast. It didn't work but he would try every time!

One time, when my brother impatiently tried to cook for himself, he boiled some hotdogs and splashed the hot water on his chest. Oh, God! I thought I would pass out, but I couldn't because my mom wasn't home, and I had to take care of him. That was what I did. I splashed cold water all over his chest to cool him down. When my mother finally got home and we took him to the emergency room, the doctor told her that I had done the best thing for him and that the cold water would help him heal. For a while after that, I would beat him every time he even spoke about cooking anything else! And whenever we had a little food left, I would make the worst dish ever…elbow macaroni and barbeque sauce! We ate it like it was steak! And just imagine, I was just nine at the time.

I was not just his sister but also like a mother. I washed our clothes in the bathtub and sent him to school clean. Well, as clean as I could! If I was lucky, when my mother was around, I could go to school too but if not, I had to stay home because I was not allowed to leave the door unlocked. One year I missed more than eighty days of school, the social worker said. What she didn't know was that I didn't want to miss school at all. Going to school was safe and, of course, school lunches were available. Most kids didn't like them but for us, it wasn't a matter of liking anything because we needed to eat. So, school was important to us!

All that was bad enough, but we also had frequent visits from a social worker who was determined to catch me in a lie. She would always come at the very time when my mother wouldn't be home. I couldn't say that she hadn't been home for a day or two, so I would say things like "You just missed her," "She just left to go to the store," or "She was rushed to the hospital and my grandmother is coming to get us." NOT! Boy, I was taught early how to lie well. I don't think she believed me, but I stuck to the story every time. And for some in that position, it was just a job, so weren't worth the extra steps to file a report against my mother. When I would tell Grandma Clark about the visits from the social worker and how I had lied to her about where my mother was, she would say "Good job!" This was because Grandma was on a mission to protect my mother at all costs too! When would someone put us first?

I thought all those things were bad enough until the day came when our apartment was raided by a group of men dressed in all-black. I remember that day more than most days because I thought we would be killed! My mother and a friend of hers were getting high in the bathroom while my brother and I were watching TV in the living room. Suddenly, men climbed through the kitchen window, broke through the back door, and kicked in the front door. They dragged my mother and her friend out of the bathroom and threw them on the floor, then tied up their hands and feet with extension cords and pointed guns at them. I guess they were there to rob them; I'm still not sure. One of the men said, "The only reason you're not dying tonight is because your kids are sitting here!" We were terrified! That changed how we thought about life going forward.

Well, the day came for my brother when one of those visits from a new social worker caused a case of neglect to be filed; he went to live with Grandma Clark in her senior citizens' building. I was left with my mother because Grandma said two women in the same house couldn't make it together; she felt like I was old enough to take care of myself. I wasn't but that was the story she told to make herself feel better. Mind you, my brother didn't have it easy there, either. Try being raised by an old lady in her then seventies with old-fashioned and new-fashioned ways all mixed together. She had too many secrets of her own and issues about controlling the people in her environment. He always had to make sure he showed her that he was grateful by being passive toward her. He had to take ridicule from her son, who was jealous of my brother for getting her attention. And guilt from my mother for leaving her. Or getting teased about his weight because now he could eat as much as he wanted but didn't know when to stop…worrying that one day he would be sent back and therefore had to store food for later. Aside from all that, my brother worked his way through Wentworth Institute to attain a degree in Computer Engineering on his own. Everyone was so proud of him and bragged about his accomplishments. The funny thing is, I was both proud and jealous of him. I had never heard that kind of praise from anyone and I wanted someone to be proud of me too.

The first time I heard Grandma Clark say she was proud of me and that I was a good mother was on her death bed. Yes, I waited years for that, and then she left us. I was about twenty-three years old with two children by then. Those words weren't enough for me at that time but later I would find peace in them because I believe she meant what she said. I've learned that people can love you only the way they know how and not the way you want them to. I have joy now because I'm proud of myself!

My brother and I had our share of troubles and good times. We both enjoyed various parts of our childhood. I can say, for myself, that I was the happiest when we were together. Though we didn't always live in the same house, we always had a sense of being together.

So, I found that sometimes your peace will come in pieces. I try to enjoy even the little things; they matter too!

CHAPTER FIVE

DOES CRIME EVER PAY?

Well, crime did sometimes pay the rent and occasionally paid the phone bills and bought us clothes and food but not really! Crime kept us dressed well, and we had computers, video games, etc., but none of it lasted very long. Crime also kept us running back and forth from Boston to New Jersey and back to Boston. You know…when there was an issue in Boston, we moved to New Jersey and so on for years. The criminal offenses were endless too! I remember going to a department store with my mother, excited because she had told us that she would get something nice for us that day. We were dressed well and we knew how to act in public, no doubt! So to the store we went, shopping, picking up all these beautiful things. Then she whispered that her name was "____" and that we had to call her that. I remember looking at her like she was crazy. She knew what was in my head and quickly reassured me that it was just a game she was playing. Once, twice, and a few hundred times more, I learned that wasn't a game at all but what would grow into a criminal enterprise. Yes, you guessed it! Identity theft was it and she was the best at it!

This business would become so big that friends, family, and neighbors would put in their orders for whatever they could think of that they wanted. This was not just a source of extra things for us. Sometimes our apartment looked like a store, with leather coats hanging on the wall and boxes with TVs stacked up for sale. She would take orders from her customers and quote prices to them. People would be in and out of our apartment buying and selling either drugs or merchandise like it was the mall. Wait! You would think she would pay the rent or buy food with that money but nope! She would even steal the very games and clothes she bought for us and sell them in the street for her drug habit. But we were supposed to believe someone had broken into the house and taken <u>only</u> those items…

During this time, my brother and I endured ridicule from some of the neighborhood parents who advised their kids not to play with us because of my mother's lifestyle, which some of them shared in but they were still able to work every day. We would get into fights with kids because they were making fun of us or my mom. It wasn't easy for us. We should have been playing, making friends, having fun, and we did at times but other times we were just trying to make it. My little brother and I would ask each other if we thought we would live to be sixteen or eighteen or twenty-one years old and what that life would look like. It seemed so far off and so impossible for us to make. From our view, we could hope to live only until the next week or the next month. We thought there were no goals or dreams for us; it was all about how to make it each day, struggling to eat, get to school, and not be taken by the welfare department. We truly thought we'd be dead by our teenage years, and we were only eight and ten years old at the time. Most kids dream about their summer plans, birthdays, and Christmas but we dreamed about food. We couldn't imagine living long!

Thank God, we lived through that and we are still living! I know now that circumstances are temporary even though it doesn't feel like that at all. And life is what I decide and not what someone else decides for me!

One time I almost paid the price for my mother's criminal behavior because I applied to become a foster parent...my *bright idea* to give back! I was told by the Department of Social Services that I could not foster a child under them. I asked why, and the woman replied, "We don't give kids to criminals." I didn't understand what she was talking about! Until then, I had never been in trouble with the law, but little did I know...I had warrants in my name! When the woman explained that I had warrants in the Worcester County courthouse for check fraud, I couldn't believe it. I tried to explain that it wasn't me but she just kept saying that it was my responsibility to fix it. I don't think she believed me. I got up the courage and asked someone to take me there. When I arrived, I was told that I could be taken into custody that day. I was shaking. I felt sick, I was sad, I was angry and maybe a little crazy! I stood before the judge and explained that they had the wrong person. It wasn't me, not me! The judge showed some compassion and asked me to come back the next day so that the store representative could identify me.

So back to the courthouse I went the next day. The store representative confirmed that it was not me, but he showed me and the judge a photo of the person, then went on to say that although he knew it was not me, the resemblance was too close. I had to know the person and if I didn't tell them who it was, I would be charged as a co-conspirator. You don't have to guess. I told them exactly who she was (my mother), where she lived, her phone number, and everything! The judge said, "I'm so sorry that this happened to you and by the person by which it came from." It was embarrassing, to say the least, but that wasn't my first time being embarrassed and not my last!

My hands weren't clean either. I remember stealing bread, lunch meat, and other things when I was little, to eat and feed my brother. I'm not proud, not bragging, but we were desperate! To me, I was a criminal too, no better than any other criminal, and that would bring me so much shame. At that time, I would do almost anything to not hear my brother cry that he was hungry!

Stealing from my mother's friends was not above me either. My excuse was that this was all their fault anyway. It wasn't altogether true, but I needed that reason to avoid feeling bad. They stole my mother from me, so I took what I needed from them while they were in the kitchen or bathroom getting high. One of them knew and never said anything. I think that's why she allowed me to work babysitting and cleaning to make money instead of stealing. I thank God for her in a way because that stopped me from continuing down that road. She would give me thirty dollars to buy milk for her and let me keep the change, telling me, "Now get you and your brother something to eat." I was so grateful to her!

Maybe, according to this woman, crime did pay…maybe some of the nice things she did for me was her way of paying back for her crimes and addiction?

CHAPTER SIX

New Jersey, Here We Come Again!

I was about ten years old when my mother moved us to Newark, New Jersey. She said we were getting a fresh start! So, she left us with my aunt until she settled things in Boston and returned to get us. She didn't! She returned to Boston and was incarcerated for eighteen months but no one knew that. In the meantime, we were living with my aunt, her friend, and two young children in the projects. My aunt also had a drug problem and it showed no mercy! I want to believe that my aunt loved us, but I didn't feel much of that love. My brother and I were older than her children by a few years and so we became responsible for them. She would disappear for days, leaving us with no food most of that time, but we found a community room in the projects where she lived that provided hot prepackaged meals three times a day. There was one issue, though. We had to get out of the apartment and that posed a problem because we couldn't open the door sometimes. My cousins were all little kids, with one in diapers and the other barely walking. It was extremely hard! We would bang on the metal door, asking whoever walked by to push the door open for us and sometimes not closing it all the way, so we could get out the next day. It was dangerous to leave the door propped open in any area but especially in the project development, though it couldn't be helped. Three times a day, seven days a week, we had to walk up and down seventeen flights of stairs if the elevator didn't work. It was our only way to eat. When my aunt was home, things were worse for my brother and me because she would buy food and snacks like cookies and fix them just right in a jar or pot, so she could tell if we ate from it. If we did, we were beaten with an extension cord. There was a time when she tied my hands to the faucet and beat me for eating more than she gave me. I never understood why…

Somehow, a neighbor in the building got in touch with my grandmother and told her what was happening, so she came to get us. That day, I thought my grandmother looked like an angel coming to rescue us. My two cousins went to stay with a family friend who took care of them until my grandmother retired and finished raising them. My brother and I went to stay with my uncle and his family for a while. Life still wasn't great, but at least it was better! We could be kids again, play and not stress…eat and not worry…sleep and not have nightmares!

That experience created a bond between my brother, myself, and my cousins. We have remained close and nothing will change that! They are my babies even though they're *old* now!

I feel like every kid deserves to be a kid!

My lesson from this is to make the best of every circumstance, no matter how ugly it looks!

CHAPTER SEVEN

YOU MIGHT AS WELL KILL ME!

Harsh isn't it? That was how I felt at the age of eighteen. It all started when I went into foster care because I confided in my sixth-grade school teacher. She was kind and caring and showed me something in her that made me trust her. Her name was Ms. Pierce. She would take me home with her sometimes, talk to me about things she had been through, and give me something to eat. There were days when she would let me stay in her classroom to concentrate on completing my assignments. One day, while we were talking, she asked me some questions about my home life. I told her **everything**! The look she gave me! With tears in her eyes, she said, "I must report this. By law, I'm required to report it. I need to know how you feel about that." I told her to report it!

It was a relief to just say it finally – "I'm hungry and I'm tired" – because by then, my brother and I were sleeping outside some nights. We would get locked out of the house if the adults were shooting up. I would have to wash our clothes in the bathtub. I was only ten years old…why me? We would be hungry for days on end.

In a calm voice, she said, "I'll take you." But that never happened because back then it wasn't allowed. Foster care, here I come. I went to court on my birthday. I will never forget that…April 1. I was turning twelve that day and all my mother said to me was "You'll be back," but I never did go back.

That right there would open the door for a so-called uncle to use me, molest me, lie to me, and abuse me, all in the name of love. That open door started right in his own mother's apartment, and she was in the living room the whole time. He started with lies that he was the only one who understood me, loved me, and was concerned about me. He told me that everyone else had given up on me because I was older than my brother and had been exposed to much more than he had; that they were afraid to take me because I would be too much trouble. So, he would buy my clothes and shoes for school. At first, I thought that was great! I needed those things and he provided them. He gave me rides to school and made sure I had a few dollars in my pocket just in case I needed lunch money. Little did I know what that open door would expose me to…

The first time he touched me, I didn't want to believe what was happening. When I told him to stop, he said, "But I love you and this is what love feels like." At that age, love felt terrible! Love felt nasty! I would never look at love the same way! That "love" caused me to become hate-filled in my attitude and how I spoke to adults. I didn't like any of them! That love disappointed me! When I was about fourteen years old, he told me he would stop when I was sixteen. Then, two years later, when I was sixteen, he told me he would stop when I got a boyfriend so that's just what I did…got a boyfriend I didn't even want! But of course, that was a lie! The story would change to "I'll stop when you become sexually active" …but that didn't stop him either! The odd thing is that I was still in foster care, but I felt like I couldn't stop going to my grandmother's house. I still wanted to be connected to my family somehow. When I think about all of this now, I sometimes get angry with myself because if I had just walked away from them all and made the best of my situation in foster care, I would have been better off. That's how I thought but I don't really know for sure what would have become of me.

    At the age of eighteen, having aged out of foster care and with no place to go, I found myself foolishly living in this man's apartment with him, his girlfriend, and his good friend. These two enabled him to continue his bad behavior. Both his girlfriend and his roommate knew what he was doing and said nothing. One night, his girlfriend caught him in my room, kneeling by my bed with his hands in my sheets, but after she confronted him the next morning and he told her off, nothing more was ever said. In fact, he made her feel like something was wrong with her and that she was stupid for bringing it up. He was sometimes emotionally abusive toward her, putting her down and making her feel incompetent about thinking for herself. I sometimes felt worse for her than I did for myself because I thought of her as weaker than I was. His *good friend* was no better. He would also sometimes catch my uncle inappropriately touching me and he said nothing!

How can you stand up to someone whom everyone else admires? All his awards for outstanding community service; numerous acknowledgments of gratitude from former drug addicts praising him; appreciating him for his help in getting them off drugs... Sometimes it made me angry; other times I was proud because I knew how far he had come in his struggle with drug addiction. Still other times it caused me to doubt what was really happening to me. So many emotions and nothing made sense. But the older I got, the less I feared him or what he said would happen to me if I reported him! Oh, I told his mother what was happening, and she said, "You're a damn liar!" That statement hurt me to my core, but I would later understand why she needed to believe that. She already had to come to grips with the fact that she had raised a liar, thief, ex-convict, and drug addict who then somewhat turned his life around. Why would she now believe that she had raised a child molester? As a parent now myself, I pity her because she would rather sacrifice me and continue living a lie. She wanted to die believing that she was free to be proud of her son; after all, she spent more than fifty years crying because of the things he would do. There's a price to be paid for a false sense of peace and the lies we tell to hold on to it.

That living situation went on for a few more months but I couldn't take it anymore, so I did the wrong thing: I lied to my friend's mother. I told her that I urgently needed to find someplace to go because my uncle was losing his apartment. Part of that was true; his girlfriend was threatening to leave him (reasons that had nothing to do with me), which would have left him homeless, but that was highly doubtful. I just needed to get away at any cost! At that point, the lie was worth being free from this man. I realized later that the truth would have been better than that lie. That I should have trusted the truth! I'm not really sure if I lied because of my shame or my pride or both. All I know is that I could no longer believe *his* lies! There was so much I didn't know, for example, that I could have stayed with my foster mother had she gotten guardianship of me or that I could have gone to college with a special grant for foster children. No one told me I had choices. I needed options!

I have learned that you can't fix a problem with a lie.

CHAPTER EIGHT
The Day I Left!

Let me go back a little. In high school, one of my friends must have told her parents about me and the problems I had. They offered to buy me a car and insured it for one year to help me because I was going to school and working two jobs. I accepted! That was my very first car: a brown Dodge Aries. That crazy car wouldn't start when it snowed! Because I had two after-school jobs and a car, and because my friend's mother gave me a place to stay, I had the courage I needed to leave my uncle completely. The day I moved out was a great day! I left work early and tried to make it home before anyone got there. I packed my stuff in that car and, with joy, left! The thing was, I didn't know that my uncle was on his way home. As I was driving, he spotted me at a red light and saw that the car was packed full. When the light turned green, he pulled his car in front of mine to block me. He got out and reached into my car to open the door, yelling, arms swinging. I was trying to roll the window up as fast as I could while yelling back, "Leave me alone," but without thinking, I put my foot on the gas and ran into his car! That's right! It felt good too!

I was free, or so I thought. Well, I was free from him and that was all that mattered to me at the time. I moved in with my friend and her family. That wasn't the answer to my problems, but it was a short-term remedy, I thought. However, I learned that even the best intentions can get a little messy. As much as my friend and her mom cared about me, she too thought I would never amount to much. That was a hard reality to face. I came to realize that the best Christmas gifts, more food than I could eat, and a nice place to live didn't change people's attitudes toward me or mine toward them. When you know how someone feels about you, sometimes it pushes you, while other times it can discourage you...it did both, to me! But I still appreciated the help! What I understood from that is nothing is FREE! Everything comes at a price and it's up to each of us to determine if whatever we're to accomplish is worth it.

Everyone has issues and problems and is simply trying to get through life. We typically think everyone else has the best life...not so! Some learn how to cover the pain better than others.

As time went on, I realized that no matter how we dress up the problem, it's still a problem and we need to deal with it. Getting away from my uncle changed my environment but not my heart or head and it certainly didn't change what folks thought about my future. You see, I wanted to go to college and become a CPA! I had dreams like everyone else! No one ever thought to ask me about mine. It's unfortunate but no one really puts too much faith in foster children, neglected children, abused children, and angry children. I was one of those children! That caused me to be disappointed by every adult in my life! I was hopeless! I just needed someone to tell me that I could make it! That I could make something out of this mess. Change was coming but I couldn't see it yet…

Now I know that freedom comes with a price! Part of being free is not worrying about the thoughts of others. I had to change what I thought about myself so that I would change my own behaviors.

CHAPTER NINE

"His Little Girl"

Funny...my dad used to call me that and I hated it at the time! What I would give to hear him call me that now. I don't talk a lot about my relationship with my father during my early years because I didn't know him then. I didn't know he existed, and I never gave it much thought. When you grow up in a neighborhood where most fathers aren't around, you don't think about it much. As I got older and asked where my father was, I was told that he was dead! I believed it. I didn't think otherwise because, I figured, why would my own mother lie? I'm not sure, even today, what that was all about. Neither my mother nor my father said much about that. I concluded it was youth and ignorance that resulted in a multitude of bad decisions, but it might have been better for me anyway.

I met him when I was about twenty years old. I was about to be a mother myself and my life would soon get more complicated. The story goes like this…my maternal grandmother went to a post office where my father's sister worked, and they recognized each other. My aunt asked my grandmother if she knew where I was. That wasn't a stupid question considering how often we moved around. My grandmother answered "yes" but explained that she had to talk to me first because at that point I was still unaware that my father existed. My grandmother thought she owed me an explanation before introducing me to him. The other issue is that I always knew my father's sister, mother, and father and considered them like family. I know it sounds strange! My mother and my aunt were extremely close when they were young women, and we all shared an apartment at one time. So, you can imagine how I felt when my grandmother, who knew all the details, told me about my father and said that he was looking for me. I was in disbelief to say the least! He had a wife and three daughters who were much younger than me. I remember the very first time I heard his voice on the phone. I had no words in my mouth. I thought it must be a mistake! From that first phone call, he called me his "little girl." Before then, I had never been anyone's "little girl."

My first visit to see him and my sisters, aunts, and cousins was awkward for me but exciting at the same time. It was awkward because, like everything else in my life, it was random, maybe accidental, or intentional; I didn't know. They all welcomed me with open arms. Still, in my disbelief, I asked him if he wanted a DNA test. He said no, that he didn't need proof. I mistakenly told my mother and other family members, thinking they might be excited and have some encouraging words for me but NO! My mother asked why he was claiming me, why he cared, and why I cared to know him. "He's not your dad," she said. My response was, "He's the only one claiming me," so now what? It was no longer just me, my mother, and my brother. I had a father, a stepmother, and sisters too. About eight years after meeting my new family members, one of my sisters passed away. I took the train to New Orleans for her service. The trip took thirty-six hours! I spent that time thinking about her, the relationship we didn't have, the memories we would never share, the stories we would never tell. It was too much for me to bear.

Until then, I had been communicating with him only by phone, so when it was time to return home, I broke down in tears, thinking I would never see him again face to face. That would be inaccurate because my dad called me every week, whether we agreed on something or not. He always insisted that we get together at someone's house or meet somewhere to vacation together. My father would always try to make things fun for his grandchildren, have talks with them, and build a relationship with them. My sisters and I would often say that no, we couldn't afford it, but then give in later and go – and I'm so glad we did! He was one of the few people in my life from whom I felt unconditional love, and it was nice.

I feel that our relationship was unique partly because we were close. We talked about everything and did not hold back on anything. We were sometimes brutally honest. However, I never called him "dad" or "daddy." Even with all the love I had for him, there was still a part of me that wasn't sure he was really my father. Plus, I had never called any man "dad" in my life! It was weird to now have to say "dad," but he never insisted on that. I didn't want to get my hopes up, trust too much, and let my heart get so involved only to be disappointed again. A year before he passed away, my sisters and I were with him in Houston, checking in on his health. I surprised him with visits like that from time to time. He was sick, and we were trying to get his health care in order. His life was starting to take back the years that he had spent abusing drugs and alcohol. My father had his issues too. He was no saint, but he had a huge heart to embrace everyone, so that made him easy to love. He considered family to be extremely important and expressed this by staying close to as much of his family as possible. One of my sisters straight out asked him if we could all take a DNA test to verify our paternity. Yup, they had their own questions too. He said, "No, wait until I die," and that was exactly what we did! One month after our visit, my dad passed away from a heart attack. A year later, I got the results of a DNA test. The good news is that I am the daughter of Lawrence Wester! I could finally shut up the voices in my head and have peace in that area. My only wish is that I felt the freedom then that I have now to let down my guard and really allow myself to be loved by him. I wish he could have heard me call him "dad"!

I have concluded that I need to make every effort to accept people for who they are and not who I want them to be. We can't choose our family, but we can choose how to love them. So, love while you can!

CHAPTER TEN
LIFE IS STILL WORTH LIVING

At about eighteen years old, I didn't think I had been given many reasons to live. I was depressed due to guilt, shame, and anger. As usual, Grandma Clark said that I would have a permanent frown on my face because I didn't smile much. I was quietly suffering! I was suicidal at that time, but no one knew. I remember feeling numb and decided that this would be the last day I felt like that! I was still living with my friend and her family. You'd think that would have been enough but it wasn't. It was a temporary fix for what felt like a lifelong heartbreak! It wasn't their fault; I felt incomplete and alone. I wasn't living with my own family, I wasn't assured that this living situation was secure, and I felt a little like an outsider looking in. As much as someone might care about you, it's not the same as having your own parents loving you.

One night, at Grandma Clark's house, I took a handful of her pills and thought I would fall asleep and die. I knew that she took high blood pressure medication and nitroglycerin (for her heart). I also thought that taking too much would cause my heart to stop, so I took them and went to sleep. I told God that if this was all there was to life, I didn't want it anymore! It wasn't worth it! I now believe that despite what I went through, despite what I did and said, God had another plan for me! He had a plan all along, but in my ignorance, I didn't know or understand that.

I woke up the next morning more disappointed than I'd been the previous morning because I thought that I couldn't even take my life right! Something was wrong with me! But GOD!

There is something that I pray every struggling young person will get early in life – something that took me years to get. That is the knowledge that, no matter what, life is worth living! No matter how bad things get, circumstances come and go but life is still worth living! Several months after that incident, I went to church with a friend, got baptized, and gave the rest of my life to God. I needed to accept that I didn't know everything, didn't understand everything, and couldn't predict anything. I was helpless, but God would make me hopeful again! I can testify that I am FULL of hope despite life's issues because I now understand that there is value in living.

Everything has worked out for my *good*. I'm living out my dreams, goals, and plans; living life daily on purpose!

Please understand that you don't need to know your future. Know that God is in your future. Just live your life and trust in the One who holds your future. Do your best in your present because your life is priceless! Take care of your mind, body, and soul because you get only one!

CHAPTER ELEVEN

This is Not The Conclusion...

I can gratefully say that the experiences I have written about are not the conclusion of my life story. I have been happily married for more than twenty-five years, with four children and a grandchild. My life is filled with family and friends, trips to foreign countries, and vacations to tropical islands. I'm enjoying making many wonderful memories. I did end up going to college while working full time and taking care of my family. It was not easy, but it was worth it and I'm benefiting now from that sacrifice. I even spent ten years studying in Bible college to increase my understanding of who God is, the depth of love He has for mankind, and His expectations about our being in a relationship with Him. That was one of my best decisions because I had to develop the person whom God created me to be and not settle for who others thought I should be.

I had to make a choice to change! I had to take some responsibility for my own mistakes, empathize about an addiction that intends to kill the person whom it has taken control of, and forgive everyone. I had to understand that forgiveness didn't let anyone off the hook but, instead, freed me to move forward in peace. I learned to love and walk away. I had to save myself before I could help anyone else. I didn't owe anyone anything that I didn't give myself first, which was respect and love. I had to learn to love myself and not attach my failures to my worth. I had to take ownership of the life God gave me and unapologetically live it!

I have expanded my mind, thoughts, and ideas by traveling and meeting different people and by experiencing various cultures and beliefs. I understand that people's experiences are different from my own, that those experiences have molded them into the person they are, and that I need to leave space for them to change too. It's become clear to me that we are not as different as we would like to believe!

I realized that I can no longer be a victim when God has made me a victor! The two are not the same. I can no longer stand by and let others dictate my future. I don't let folks push around anymore! Or believe that I'm not good enough to meet my goals. I must take self-inventory on a regular basis – tell some truths about myself and work on me!

I can say with certainty that the owner of my life (God) has made changes that I can't completely put into words. I pray that for you. I pray that you come to understand the need, to know God and love Him because He loves you. I pray that you believe His promise from 1 Corinthians 2:9: "However, as it is written: "What no eye has seen, what no ear has heard, and what no human mind has conceived" the things God has prepared for those who love him." (NIV). God has plans for you and they will absolutely blow your mind and the minds of others! So, don't give up! Be encouraged that your dreams aren't big enough to match His plans for you. I am a *living* witness!

Jeremiah 29:11 "For I know the plans I have for you," declarers the Lord, "plans to prosper you and not to harm you, plants to give you hope and a future." (NIV).

CHAPTER TWELVE

I'm Getting My Voice Back

Finally, after years of not speaking much, not hearing my own voice, sometimes for days, because I was extremely angry and had no idea what to do with that anger. When I did speak, it was from a negative place, so my words weren't received. Most of the time, I felt misunderstood, almost like I was speaking a foreign language or something. What words could I say that would effectively express all that was going through my heart and mind? How could I make anyone understand that most days I wanted to scream or just run and not stop? When would they get it? When would things change for me?

So, I went through most of my life outwardly behaving as though I cared about nothing and no one. That was a big lie. I did care a lot! I tried my best to disrupt whatever peace my grandmother or other family members had because I had no peace. I so badly wanted someone to ask me, "What's wrong?" and then make a point to listen. I wanted someone to relate to my pain; to cry with me or just hold me. Instead, I was told that I was ungrateful, mean, and disrespectful, that I would turn out just like my mother! Were those words supposed to help me or further hurt me? They hurt more than I could say!

At some point, after turning forty years old, I decided that I had to be the change that I expected to see in others. I not only began to speak but did so from a very different place even if it wasn't my reality yet. I also realized that in getting my voice back, I had to use it responsibly. I had to think about what and how I spoke. I never wanted to inflict on someone else the same pain that had been inflicted on me! So, it is a daily exercise in being thoughtful about my words because words have power! Most importantly, I use the words I speak to encourage myself and speak life to others. You know the saying: "If you don't have anything nice to say, don't say anything at all." It's true and it's a choice!

Now, I accept that no words could really define my broken heart or the level of depression that I was dealing with at that time. I needed new words to think about. In turn, I would have new words to speak over my life. When I was young, there was a saying: "Sticks and stones may break my bones but words will never hurt me!" Well, I'm here to tell you that some words do hurt you and may even affect how you think about yourself! As a mother, those words had me up at 5 a.m. cooking, mopping floors, working all day. At night, I would cook, clean, and go over and above in taking care of my family because I didn't want the words "You will be just like your mother" to ever be true! You might think that I was simply doing what I was supposed to do, and I agree with that but with one exception: Sometimes I was too tired to pay attention to the little things that matter when you have a family. The words people spoke over me dictated my decisions and how I thought about myself and the family that I was trying to care for. I was always trying to prove myself…"I'll show them!" And I did, but I would become frustrated because, to some, my efforts would never be enough. Now I live from a place of balance, caring for myself, family, church, and community, understanding that each has an equal place in my life. It's not easy but it's necessary.

At last, I'm free to live my life the way it was intended…with purpose! You see, I have the freedom to make good choices, a voice to express my feelings (good or bad), a healed heart to move beyond my past, and a new determination to see other young people get to the same point. Getting my voice back is not enough. I want to use my voice to help others take back their voices (power) to speak and live on purpose.

CHAPTER THIRTEEN

DON'T JUST SETTLE

For many years I settled for what I thought I deserved. When it came to kids with my background, I thought the way that many people think. Kids who are neglected and abused. Kids who are in the foster care system. Without realizing it, I started believing the things that people said about me; that I would not amount to much; that I was damaged goods and that it was too late for me. I started living out those thoughts by not expecting much out of life. I let go of my dream of attending college, getting a degree, and obtaining a good job. For years, I didn't celebrate my birthday because I didn't think it was a big deal. I didn't celebrate my accomplishment of getting through school; I didn't think anyone would care. I didn't give much attention to my looks, my hair, and my clothes because I didn't want to draw attention to myself. I felt that people thought that I deserved what happened to me. I didn't share my dreams and ideas with anyone because who was I to dream that big? So, I led a life in the shadows of others, slipping little bits of myself in their world, trying to fit in. It didn't work. It never will because we're not made to be someone's shadow – and no one needs a shadow anyway!

Be determined! I had to find out the long and hard way that I was more than a mere image of someone else's life. I had to understand that settling just made me increasingly frustrated and angry. Settling was no longer an option for me. I became determined to be the best me! Little by little, I changed my mind in terms of how I viewed myself. I started making plans even though I kept most of them to myself in case I failed. I could now see myself doing more, getting more, and experiencing more in life. I still quietly live out my dreams and aspirations but with a very different attitude…a "nothing can stop me now" attitude! Nothing can stop you either if you remain *determined* to not settle for anything less than your best! Just to clarify, everyone won't appreciate the new you! They might not want to hear the vocal you! Some might not even want to see the beautiful and confident you! Be you anyway!

Now, when you get free…be someone else's freedom! Don't just live your life for yourself. Give back to the community that gave to you. Give of yourself to someone who needs to know that they can make it too! Your giving doesn't just look like money; it can be your time, your compassion, your words of encouragement, or your story. Our life stories are not just for us alone because someone needs to hear our testimony. I hope you know that we're not lucky…we're blessed!

CHAPTER FOURTEEN

MY FAVORITE BIBLE STORY

In Daniel chapter 3 there is an interesting story about three Hebrew boys; Shadrach, Meshach, and Abed-nego. The story describes a wicked king, Nebuchadnezzar, who ruled over Babylon. He decided to build a large statue (idol) made of gold. Nebuchadnezzar wanted it set up in the middle of Babylon for everyone to see and worship. He called on all the governors and treasurers (important people) to dedicate this statue for worship. The king declared that everyone had to bow down and worship this idol or be put to death! Daniel 3:4-6: "O peoples, nations, and languages, that at the time you hear the sound of the horn, flute, harp, lyre and psaltery, in symphony with all kinds of music, you shall fall down and worship the gold image that King Nebuchadnezzar has set up, and whoever doesn't fall down and worship shall be cast immediately into the midst of a burning fiery furnace." (NKJV).

Well, these three boys respected the king but refused to worship his god. They believed in their God only and trusted Him. When the people saw that they would not worship the king's idol, they reported the boys to the king. They were immediately taken to the king to explain why they refused to bow down and worship his god. They told the king that they could not do this because they worshipped their God only. The king gave them one last opportunity to change their minds, but they did not and were threatened with being thrown in a furnace and put to death. Daniel 3:17-18: "if that is the case, our God whom we serve is able to deliver us from the burning fiery furnace, and He will deliver us from your hand, O king. But if not, let it be known to you, O king, that we do not serve your gods, nor will we worship the gold image which you have set up." (NKJV). This angered the king, so he gave orders to not only put them to death, but to make the furnace seven times hotter than usual. The guards threw the boys in the furnace with their pants, head wraps, and other clothing still on. The furnace was so hot that it killed the guards who threw the boys inside it. Then the king noticed that there were not just the three boys walking around in the furnace but four people...one of whom looked like the son of God! These men came walking out of the furnace and were not burned; their hair was not singed; their clothes were not affected, and they did not smell of smoke! They were unharmed, so the king declared that no one could speak against their God!

I love this story because it talks about how far troubles and issues can take you; how deep faith will find you and how God's love will rescue you. This story is me! I had lots of problems, too many disappointments to count, and a good reason to give up. A little faith in God and understanding that He did love me made all the difference! I made it out, I overcame my obstacles, and my life has never been the same. God loves you too. Despite your problems...He still loves you! Despite your mistakes, failures, lack of faith...He still loves you! This story describes just how far God will go to bring you out! He can save you from what is meant to kill you! He's waiting to turn your life around and make you *new*. Give Him a chance and, like me, He will make a great testimony out of you. People will say, "You don't look like what you've been through," and, like me...you will agree!

CHAPTER FIFTEEN

YOUR BEST REVENGE!

Work on you!...

List your disappointments, hurts, and struggles and understand that they are all temporary...nothing lasts forever!

Now pray and ask God for forgiveness and the ability to forgive. You can't expect what you can't give; you can't give what you don't have...just simply say what's on your heart. Romans 12:21, "Do not be overcome by evil, but overcome evil with good." (KJV). Forgiveness is key to moving forward toward freeing yourself from the past. Forgiveness was difficult for me and came at a high price, which was feeling like the person who needed forgiving didn't deserve it. I learned something about myself...I too had to be forgiven! I had to forgive myself for allowing hate and anger to take up space in my head and heart. I had to forgive myself for feeling like I had allowed certain things to happen, like being molested by a family member. I blamed myself for not being good enough, for needing to be in foster care and not being with my family. While raising my children, I wasted time trying to prove that I wasn't my mom instead of enjoying the experience of BEING a mom.

There were so many mistakes, misunderstandings, miscommunications, and missed opportunities on my part...things that I held onto and had to forgive myself for first. Know what it feels like to be forgiven by yourself first. Then you will understand how much better you will feel when you forgive someone else. You free yourself from holding the weight, luggage, and issues that are setting you back. It's more important to succeed than it is to hold unnecessary stuff. For example, every few months or so I take everything out of my closets, look through every single piece of clothing, shoes, etc., and throw away the stuff I hadn't used or didn't need maybe because it's old and outdated or maybe because I no longer need it because I've replaced it with something better. What's in the closet of your heart? What can you get rid of? What can you replace with something better, healthier? Make room for a better, healthier life filled with joy and peace.

Often, we think of revenge as something negative but revenge can be positive in the sense that our forgiving and letting go of every disappointment, discouragement, failure, and pain will cause you to see yourself differently, therefore causing others to see you differently too. You are becoming new! Letting go will make room for a new way of thinking, new experiences, new people, and new opportunities. Being filled with the old leaves no room for the NEW!

Now set your goals, write your dreams, and make some plans…include God! Proverbs 16:9, "A man's heart plans his way, but the Lord directs his steps." (NKVJ). You may not accept this point now but hopefully you will in time. He needs to be in your plans and dreams.

Setting and sharing goals with a trusted family member or friend is essential because it makes you accountable to someone. Set goals to recognize that you have work to do for yourself. These goals must challenge you to work harder, strive for better, and see yourself higher. Don't just settle…I did that because I didn't see my value except through someone else's view and I hurt myself in the process. Know the difference between arrogance and self-confidence. Arrogance says, "I know everything, especially about myself!" It's having an exaggerated feeling of importance. "Everyone is beneath me!" Self-confidence says, "I'm grateful for my accomplishments but am open to learning more. I trust my abilities and judgment." Now, I want to introduce you to God-confidence. This confidence is totally in God, accepting how much He loves you, understanding the lengths He went to so that He could provide another way for you, and He has plans for your success. When you have God-confidence, you trust a limitless God, which means His plans can't fail! Having God-confidence and not religion will take you further than your own physical strength. Jeremiah 29:11: "For I know the plans I have for you, declares the Lord, plans to prosper you and not to harm you, plans to give you hope and a future." (NIV). You need this!

Get ready for the new. You've held on to the old long enough and your past is never worth sacrificing your future!

This girl has overcome, this is my best revenge...You can overcome too!

Acknowledgements

I just want to say, "Thank you!" I can't close this book without saying thank you to my husband and children: You gave me a reason to get up every morning and give my best! You loved me even when you didn't understand me and waited for me to figure out what I was doing. You followed me and supported me unconditionally…I love you! To my siblings…what a roller coaster ride we have been on! My only brother and friend: We have been through so much, but we have made it, always remembering the message to stick together. My sisters and cheerleaders: You both uniquely impress me with how you live your best life! I'm more than proud of all of you…

I think you're, without a doubt, the best!

To all my friends who helped me throughout my life in one way or another: You played a major role in assisting me in getting to this point in my journey and it's not over! No matter how big or small you think your contribution was, believe me when I say that it made an impact. Your patience with me during my various transitions in life made it easier.

Acknowledgements

To my church <u>families</u>: There are too many to name you all, but you know who you are. I have learned and accomplished so much in ministry because you trusted and worked with me. You tolerated my bossiness and pushed me beyond my comfort zone. Somehow, many of you understood me and my passion to do more in the community. You made room for me.

I am so grateful!

Now, with all that being said, I owe the biggest thank you to my Lord, Jesus Christ. Without Your help, where would I be? At my most desperate times, I called on You; You heard me and came to rescue me. Even when I made mistake after mistake, trying to fix my own way, You were there to encourage me. Your never-ending love for me is teaching me how to love others the same way. Your compassion toward what hurts me has enabled me to have compassion toward others in ways that most don't understand. Your promise to me…"to never leave me or forsake me"…has proved to me that You will never disappoint me! Your healing virtue has covered me. It continues to heal me and make me whole. You always assure me that "your plans for me are good, not evil and have an expected end"; I can rely on You. Your grace in my life empowers me, gives me spiritual authority, and has favored me and amazed me in understanding that because of You, I can't fail. Your divine protection has relieved me of all my fears and left me with peace and joy. Your blessings have overtaken me. I am living in overflow now. You have forgiven me, corrected me, taught me, and promoted me. You have done for me what no man could ever do. Your commitment to me has caused me to trust and love You more!

ACKNOWLEDGEMENTS

Lastly, because you have been a faithful Father, I no longer walk in fear! I no longer lay in self-doubt! I no longer need the approval of others! I no longer fear the truth! I no longer run from change! I am no longer quietly dying inside!

Because of You, this woman is an OVERCOMER!

About The Author

My name is Tawanna Monique Jackson-Adams and I have been married to my husband for 28 years. I have four adult children and one granddaughter.

I attended Newbury College, where I majored in Medical Administration, while also studying at Covenant Christian Ministries, Bethel Bible Institute, and Ezra Bible Institute.

Currently, I am employed at Cambridge Associates as a Senior Administrative Assistant. There, I also serve on multiple committees such as the Administrative Training Team and CA Women's Development Team.

In 2019, I founded and became President of God C.A.R.E.S. Inc., a nonprofit organization that educates and encourages foster children to pursue the resources available to them in the community; supply personal toiletry bags to individuals without housing; "Gabby's Gifts" giving struggling families with children a smile during the holidays and an annual "Celebration of Victory" cancer care charity event to provide cancer patients and their families with items needed to make getting treatment a little easier.

About The Author

In addition, I serve as the Director of Ministries at Edify Church Boston, where I find joy in mentoring the leadership staff to always give God their best through skill development, prayer, and personal integrity.

As a travel agent with a thriving business that specializes in group cruise and resort trips, I have an opportunity to encourage individuals/families to travel beyond the "norm" and gain exposure to new and exciting adventures. I am grateful that I can give the gift of travel to those I love and some who have now become like family to me.

My goal is to serve God and His people well in all that I do! I have a strong passion for seeing people prosper in every area of their lives; to be whole and experience the best that life has to offer by understanding the depth of God's love for us; and to use my life as just one example of what God's amazing grace looks like.

My greatest achievement is my relationship with God and my family – neither of which is perfect by itself but that, together, are awesome! I can also say that embracing forgiveness, understanding what love really is, and accepting my God-given assignment for my life have given me great joy. My husband would say that I watch too much HGTV, which gives me more ideas than he would like!

www.ingramcontent.com/pod-product-compliance
Lightning Source LLC
Chambersburg PA
CBHW041131110526
44592CB00020B/2770